THE STORY OF
POP MUSIC

POP HISTORIES

MATT ANNISS

A+

Smart Apple Media

Published in the United States by Smart Apple Media
PO Box 3263, Mankato, Minnesota 56002

Text: Matt Anniss
Editors: Joe Harris and Rachel Blount
Design: Paul Myerscough and Keith Williams

Picture credits:
Corbis: Bettmann 10t, Earl & Nazima Kowall 17t, Ross Marino/Sygma 19b, Robert Matheu/Retna Ltd. 9t, Michael Ochs Archives 12, Denis O'Regan 21; Dreamstime: Kristina Afanasyeva 28, Imagecollect 18; Getty Images: CBS Photo Archive 6r, Hulton Archive 13b; Library of Congress: William P. Gottlieb Collection 5b; Shutterstock: Christian Bertrand 31, S Bukley 5t, 13t, DFree 25t, 26l, Dotshock 4, Helga Esteb 24, 26r, Featureflash 1, 20b, 23b, 25b, 29l, Jaguar PS 19t, Patricia Marks 11t, Music4mix 22, Joe Seer 23t, 27, 29r; Wikia.com: ReapTheChaos 8; Wikipedia: Archivey 16, Beaucoupkevin 17b, CBS Television 6l, 15b, Colgems Records 9b, Angela George 11b, Goaliej54 20t, Roland Godefroy 7, Jimieye 17c, Heinrich Klaffs 14, Robert L. Knudsen 15t.
Cover images: Amazon: top center right; Shutterstock: Efecreata Photography top far left, Featureflash top center left, Pressmaster main, Debby Wong top left; Wikipedia: CBS Television top far right, Colgems Records top right.

Library of Congress Cataloging-in-Publication Data

Anniss, Matt.
The story of pop music / Matt Anniss.
     pages cm. -- (Pop histories)
 Includes index.
Summary: "Describes the world of pop music, explaining how the music evolved and spotlighting its different eras and important musicians"--Provided by publisher.
ISBN 978-1-59920-970-8 (library binding)
1. Popular music--History and criticism--Juvenile literature. I. Title.
ML3470.A58 2014
781.63--dc23
                                 2013003183

Printed in China

SL002671US

Supplier 03, Date 0513, Print Run 2378

CONTENTS

THE PREHISTORY OF POP

The story of pop music is the history of the changes in attitudes and technology that defined the twentieth century. It touches on other forms of entertainment, fashion, and fads. More than anything, it is the story of music that people love.

Vaudeville

Up until the early part of the twentieth century, the only way to enjoy music was to listen to it being played live. One of the most popular styles of entertainment at the time was "vaudeville". Vaudeville shows mixed performances of popular songs, comedy, and dance.

TIN PAN ALLEY

The popularity of vaudeville created a demand for new songs that could be performed by the scene's top singers. Because of this, a thriving songwriting industry developed. In the United States, it was based around a street in New York nicknamed "Tin Pan Alley".

Recorded Music

In the early part of the twentieth century, two inventions began to change the nature of the popular music scene. The first was the gramophone, a machine that allowed people to listen to music recorded to pressed plastic discs, known as records, in their own home. The second was the radio.

THE GRAMOPHONE, WHICH HELPED POPULARIZE RECORDED MUSIC IN THE EARLY TWENTIETH CENTURY, WAS THE FORERUNNER OF THE RECORD "DECKS" USED BY CLUB DJs.

Radio Stars

Until cheaper record players became available in the 1950s, radio was the most popular way of listening to music. Top singers from the vaudeville scene could become big stars if they featured on the radio. Being on the radio helped to sell concert tickets.

THE FIRST POP STAR

Radio helped make Frank Sinatra the world's first pop star. During the 1940s, Sinatra's records sold in huge numbers. He was a larger-than-life character with a distinctive singing style. He was so popular that he soon started appearing in movies.

Groundbreaking Star

Sinatra was hugely popular with teenagers, who had previously shown little interest in music. It was a groundbreaking change. In years to come, teenagers would become the driving force behind pop music.

SINGER FRANK SINATRA WAS ONE OF POP MUSIC'S FIRST GLOBAL STARS AND WENT ON TO STAR IN A NUMBER OF SUCCESSFUL MOVIES.

5

ROCK AROUND THE CLOCK

Frank Sinatra may have been the world's first pop star, but pop music as we know it began in the 1950s. DJ Alan Freed began using the term "rock and roll" to describe the music he broadcast, the decade's most popular form of music.

Rockin' Revolution

Rock and roll was different to other forms of popular music that had come before. It was loud, energetic, dancefloor-friendly, and was based on African-American music styles such as rhythm and blues and jazz. In the mid 1950s, it emerged from America and took the world by storm.

At the Movies

It wasn't a particular song or singer that popularized rock and roll. Instead, it was through the movies *Blackboard Jungle* (1955) and *Rock Around the Clock* (1956) that most teenagers discovered rock and roll.

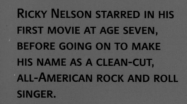

RICKY NELSON STARRED IN HIS FIRST MOVIE AT AGE SEVEN, BEFORE GOING ON TO MAKE HIS NAME AS A CLEAN-CUT, ALL-AMERICAN ROCK AND ROLL SINGER.

FOLLOWING THE SUCCESS OF HIS FIRST SINGLE, *THAT'S ALRIGHT MAMA* IN 1954, ELVIS PRESLEY QUICKLY BECAME KNOWN AS "THE KING OF ROCK AND ROLL".

Sales Boom

Rock and roll was the first style of popular music to increase the sales of both record players and the records themselves. Teenagers wanted to be able to listen to their favorite rock and roll songs at home. Record shops began to appear all over the United States.

Singles Life

In the past, records had been expensive and didn't sound very good. Thanks to the recent invention of the 7-inch single—a cheap record featuring one song per side of the disc—rock and roll records could be made, sold, and bought cheaply. Sales of records skyrocketed.

POP CHARTS

During the 1950s and early 1960s, the music industry grew faster than at any stage before or since. To keep track of record sales, pop charts were set up. Like they do today, the pop charts listed the top-selling singles.

First Pop Hit

America's first number one was *Poor Little Fool* by Ricky Nelson. It topped the Billboard Hot 100 in August 1958. Since then, over 1,000 different songs have topped the American pop charts.

PLAYLIST
1950s POP MUSIC

Bill Haley & the Comets —*Rock Around the Clock* (1955)

Elvis Presley—*All Shook Up* (1957)

Ricky Nelson—*Poor Little Fool* (1958)

Chuck Berry—*Johnny B. Goode* (1958)

Johnny Horton—*The Battle of New Orleans* (1959)

THANKS TO CATCHY SONGS SUCH AS *JOHNNY B. GOODE*, CHUCK BERRY BECAME ONE OF THE FIRST AFRICAN-AMERICAN ROCK AND ROLL STARS.

ON THE TUBE

The popularity of music with teenagers during the early years of pop made TV producers sit up and take notice. TV was still in its early years but gaining in popularity. Soon, TV would play a huge role in creating pop stars.

Good for Everyone

In the 1950s, TV producers were looking for ways to attract more viewers to their shows. Booking pop acts made sense, since it guaranteed that teenagers would tune in. It was good also for the pop acts, since millions of potential record buyers would hear their songs.

VARIETY SHOWS

To start with, pop acts began appearing on popular variety shows, which mixed singing and dancing with comedy and impressions. It wasn't long, though, before TV networks began to set up their own dedicated music shows aimed at teenagers.

The Forerunner of MTV

Fronted by a former radio DJ named Dick Clark, *American Bandstand* was the world's first dedicated pop music TV show. It first aired on ABC in 1957 and featured teenagers dancing to pop records and performances from leading singers.

MANY TEENAGERS BECAME INTERESTED IN ROCK AND ROLL AFTER SEEING BILL HALEY AND THE COMETS PERFORM ON TV.

Top of the Pops

The success of *American Bandstand* inspired a British version called *Top of the Pops*. Both shows played a key role in promoting pop music to TV viewers over the next 40 years.

Star Makers

Appearing on TV shows had the potential to turn pop acts into huge stars, particularly in the United States. The Beatles become stars in America almost overnight following their appearance on *The Ed Sullivan Show* in 1964.

Monkee Magic

The runaway success of pop group the Beatles inspired a 1960s U.S. TV comedy about a band called *The Monkees*. Although musical, the four members of the band were hired as actors, but the songs they recorded for the show went on to be huge pop hits.

PRESENTER DICK CLARK, SHOWN HERE WITH BAND THE GO-GO'S, BECAME ONE OF THE MOST FAMOUS FACES IN AMERICA THANKS TO HOSTING THE POP MUSIC TV SHOW *AMERICAN BANDSTAND*.

LIVING LEGENDS

THE MONKEES

At the height of their fame, the Monkees were the most popular pop band on the planet. After beginning life as a group of actor/musicians, they eventually became a full-fledged pop band that recorded songs and performed concerts. To date, they've sold 65 million records.

GIRLS AND BOYS

The 1960s was a golden age for pop music. It was also a golden age for the star-makers— the managers, songwriters, and music producers who worked hard behind the scenes to turn bands and singers into stars.

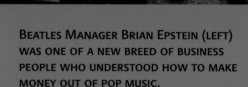

BEATLES MANAGER BRIAN EPSTEIN (LEFT) WAS ONE OF A NEW BREED OF BUSINESS PEOPLE WHO UNDERSTOOD HOW TO MAKE MONEY OUT OF POP MUSIC.

Shining Stars

In the 1960s, pop groups were much more popular than singers. Being in a pop group was not a guarantee of success, though. To become stars, you needed a good manager and a record producer who would make your songs sound good.

TOP MANAGER

The most successful pop manager of all was Brian Epstein, the man who turned the Beatles into the biggest band on the planet. Epstein knew that the Beatles sounded good, but to succeed, they'd also need to look good on TV.

The Importance of Image

Epstein and other 1960s pop managers understood that "image", or how a band looked, was an important part of their appeal to teenagers. Because of this, managers concentrated just as much on how a band looked as how they sounded.

Let's Go Surfing

The Beach Boys, one of the most popular groups of the 1960s, took pride in their appearance. Their smart-casual look matched their songs, which were mostly about girls, cars, and surfing. Their all-American sound and look appealed to their teenage audience.

Motown Sound

To help them sound good, 1960s pop groups worked with the best record producers. Norman Whitfield and Berry Gordy, Jr., the men behind the Motown record label, understood this more than most. Between them, they produced hundreds of hit singles, almost single-handedly turning pop fans on to soul music.

INSIDE THE SOUND

BEAT MUSIC

The most popular form of pop music in Britain in the early 1960s was "beat music", a sound made popular by groups such as the Beatles. Based around a steady beat, its catchy songs combined rock and roll guitars with pop singing styles, sometimes influenced by American soul.

HITSVILLE U.S.A. IN DETROIT, THE ORIGINAL HOME OF SOUL RECORD LABEL MOTOWN, IS NOW A POPULAR MUSEUM.

FORMER SONGWRITER BERRY GORDY, JR. UNDERSTOOD HOW TO MAKE POP RECORDS AND TURNED HIS COMPANY, MOTOWN RECORDS, INTO A HUGE BUSINESS EMPIRE.

The Hit Factory

Motown was one of the first pop "hit factories" around. The company used the same musicians and producers to record songs with different singers, guaranteeing a consistent "sound". Today, hit factories are still an essential part of the pop music scene.

11

POP ART

By the mid-1960s, pop music was growing up. While the charts were still full of short, catchy songs, many pop groups and singers had a desire to make more substantial music. Pop was becoming art.

Battle of the Bands

Two of the world's biggest pop bands, the Beatles and the Beach Boys, led this change. Both groups were interested in other styles of music and wanted to include new sounds in their songs. So they set about trying to reflect all of these influences in their music.

WITH THEIR *PET SOUNDS* ALBUM, THE BEACH BOYS TURNED THEIR BACK ON SURFING-INSPIRED POP IN FAVOR OF SONGS THAT WERE MUCH MORE MUSICALLY COMPLEX.

Studio Time

By 1966, the Beatles had decided to stop playing concerts. Instead, they spent more time at Abbey Road recording studios with record producer George Martin. They wanted to create a pop album that featured songs in many different styles, from folk-rock and Motown-style soul to tracks influenced by experimental classical music composers.

LANDMARK ALBUM

When it was released in 1966, the Beatles' *Revolver* album was hailed as a masterpiece. It didn't sound like any other pop album that had been made before. It used Indian instruments, soul-style horns, backward guitar solos, and special effects to enhance the sound.

Beat It

Revolver wasn't the only landmark album released in 1966. The Beach Boys' *Pet Sounds* set new standards for how pop albums were recorded and was every bit as adventurous as *Revolver*. It's still thought of as one of the best albums of all time.

Classic Pop

In 1967, the Beatles raised the bar again with their most famous album, *Sgt. Pepper's Lonely Hearts Club Band*. Recorded over six months in Abbey Road, *Sgt. Pepper* was the most inventive pop album ever made. Like *Pet Sounds*, it used sounds that had never been heard before on pop records—a full orchestra, inventive recording techniques, and even fair organs.

PAUL McCARTNEY ON THE BEACH BOYS

"*Pet Sounds* by the Beach Boys blew me out of the water. It might be going overboard to say it's a classic of the twentieth century, but to me it's almost unbeatable."

Paul McCartney (pictured)

Art Attack

Sgt. Pepper and *Pet Sounds* started a trend for recording musically more interesting pop albums. They also proved, once and for all, that pop music could be about much more than just simple, radio-friendly songs.

BY TURNING THEIR BACK ON PLAYING LIVE TO SPEND MORE TIME IN THE RECORDING STUDIO, THE BEATLES CHANGED THE FACE OF POP MUSIC FOREVER.

THE AGE OF GLAMOUR

As the 1960s turned to the 1970s, the pop art of the Beach Boys and the Beatles was replaced by new pop music trends. With many older pop bands now making rock records, new pop stars emerged to entertain teenagers.

HIGH ROLLERS

Some things didn't change, though. Many of the top pop groups of the period were carefully managed and promoted to appeal to teenagers. One band that made their mark was the Bay City Rollers, a Scottish group who started a craze among their fans for wearing tartan scarves and hats.

Glam It Up

During the 1970s, the pop charts were dominated by a handful of new musical styles inspired by very different music. There was glam rock, a stomping new fusion of rock and pop, and disco, a style that emerged from the nightclubs of America to take the world by storm.

Family Affair

Groups made up of family members were also popular. The Osmonds, Carpenters, Bee Gees—and in the UK, the Nolans—were made up of brothers and sisters. All were hugely successful, dominating the pop charts on both sides of the Atlantic.

THE OSMONDS WERE A FAMILY OF PERFORMERS FROM OGDEN, UTAH. THEY WERE ONE OF THE MOST POPULAR BANDS OF THE 1970S.

BROTHER-AND-SISTER ACT THE CARPENTERS WERE ONE OF THE MOST-PLAYED POP ACTS ON AMERICAN RADIO IN THE 1970S.

PLAYLIST

1970s POP

The Jackson 5—*I'll Be There* (1970)
The Osmonds—*One Bad Apple* (1971)
The Carpenters—*We've Only Just Begun* (1970)
Bay City Rollers—*Saturday Night* (1975)
Bee Gees—*Jive Talking* (1975)

Fast Forward

Pop music has always reflected musical trends, so it wasn't long before disco dominated the pop charts. For the first time, dance music was leading pop forward into a new age.

WE ARE FAMILY

Another family group that enjoyed huge success in the 1970s was the Jackson 5. Signed to pop hit factory Motown, the five brothers made fun, feel-good soul music that people could dance to. As the 1970s progressed, they helped introduce disco to pop audiences.

DURING THE DISCO ERA IN THE LATE 1970S, THE JACKSON 5 ENJOYED MORE NUMBER ONE HITS THAN ANY OTHER SOUL BAND.

Dance to the Music

Disco was an energetic, nightclub-friendly version of soul that had started life in the underground clubs of New York. As nightclubs began to spread around the world in the mid 1970s, dancing to disco records became wildly popular.

THE NEW WAVE SCENE

By the early 1980s, disco had died and glam rock was a distant memory. In place of both came another style of popular music originally inspired by dance music culture, New Wave, also known as synth-pop.

Start the Dance

As the 1970s turned to the 1980s, dance music producers began using new, cutting-edge electronic instruments such as synthesizers and drum machines. These allowed musicians and producers to create futuristic sounds and tracks.

Industrial Roots

Pop music created using synthesizers first emerged from European cities such as Dusseldorf and Sheffield in the mid 1970s. To begin with, though, it was largely made by experimental acts with an interest in the potential of cutting-edge technology. By the early 1980s, though, synthesizer use was much more widespread and New Wave/synth-pop was quickly gaining in popularity.

STEEL CITY

Sheffield, an industrial city in the north of England, was home to many of the New Wave scene's leading acts. The Human League, Heaven 17, and ABC all enjoyed great success in the pop charts during the early part of the 1980s, having originally started out making experimental electronic music.

ABC WERE ONE OF A NUMBER OF SUCCESSFUL NEW WAVE BANDS TO EMERGE FROM THE NORTHERN ENGLISH CITY OF SHEFFIELD, WHICH WAS PREVIOUSLY FAMOUS FOR PRODUCING STEEL.

American Scene

The American dance scene, previously the birthplace of disco, also had a huge influence on the New Wave sound of the 1980s. Madonna, now one of the most successful pop singers of all time, got her break singing in underground dance clubs in New York, and Prince started out playing in underground funk and disco bands in his hometown of Minneapolis.

Dance-Pop

The sounds of underground American and European dance music also had an influence on two of the most successful British New Wave/synth-pop acts of the 1980s, Wham! and Pet Shop Boys. Both worked with top U.S. dance producers, gaining popularity in the clubs before breaking into the pop charts.

AMERICAN R & B STAR PRINCE TURNED TO THE NEW WAVE SOUND IN THE 1980S AND BECAME ONE OF THE MOST RECOGNIZABLE ARTISTS ON THE PLANET.

LIVING LEGENDS

PET SHOP BOYS

Formed in 1984 in London by former rock journalist Neil Tennant and architecture student Chris Lowe, Pet Shop Boys are the most successful pop duo of all time in the UK. Famed for their love of outrageous costumes, they have sold over 50 million records worldwide since 1985.

VIDEO KILLED THE RADIO STAR

In the 1960s and 1970s, TV had the power to make or break pop careers thanks to shows such as *American Bandstand*. In the 1980s, the relationship continued to blossom. The era of music television had arrived.

I Want My MTV

In 1981, some TV executives in upstate New York decided to launch a new cable TV station called MTV. Based around the idea of playing nonstop music videos, it would quickly go on to be the world's first 24-hour music TV station. It would also change pop music forever.

Right Place, Right Time

MTV came at the right time. The first music video shown by the station, *Video Killed the Radio Star* by British act Buggles, perfectly summed up the mood of the time. Music videos were now the most important tool for promoting pop acts around the world.

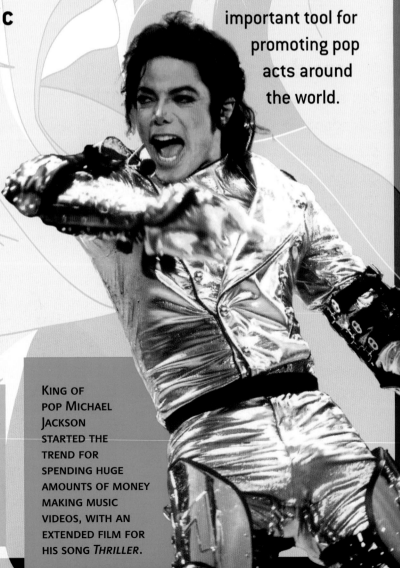

KING OF POP MICHAEL JACKSON STARTED THE TREND FOR SPENDING HUGE AMOUNTS OF MONEY MAKING MUSIC VIDEOS, WITH AN EXTENDED FILM FOR HIS SONG *THRILLER*.

THE VIDEO AGE

Music videos were not a new concept. As far back as the 1960s, popular bands such as the Beatles would record short movies to promote their songs. By 1981, more and more pop acts were recording music videos.

Pop TV

MTV was almost an overnight success. Teenagers, the core market for pop groups, would spend hours every day watching a constant stream of brand new music videos. To stand out from the crowd, it was vital for pop groups to make ever more elaborate and expensive videos.

Trendsetters

The two biggest pop stars of the 1980s, Madonna and Michael Jackson, embraced this change. Their record labels spent huge amounts of money making their videos, in the hope that they would create a stir. Jackson's *Thriller* video, which featured him dancing with a troupe of zombies, cost an astonishing $500,000.

BIG BUDGETS

Thirty years later, record labels still spend huge amounts of money creating awesome music videos for their biggest pop acts. The promotional clip for Madonna's 2012 song *Give Me All Your Loving* cost a cool $1.5 million.

POP HEROES

RIHANNA ON MADONNA

"Madonna is a great inspiration. She has reinvented her clothing style and music with success so many times, remaining a real force in entertainment."

Rihanna (pictured)

MADONNA WORKED WITH TOP FASHION DESIGNERS TO MAKE SURE THAT SHE HAD AN EXCITING NEW LOOK FOR EACH MUSIC VIDEO SHE MADE.

WHEN WILL I BE FAMOUS?

The dawn of 24-hour music television didn't just make stars of New Wave/synth-pop acts with an eye for fashionable clothes. It also saw the return of "manufactured" pop groups put together by ambitious managers.

Mixed Audience

Although stars such as Madonna and Michael Jackson appealed to teenagers, they had older followers. The same wasn't true for many manufactured acts of the late '80s and early '90s. These attractive young people were chosen by managers to appeal to teenagers.

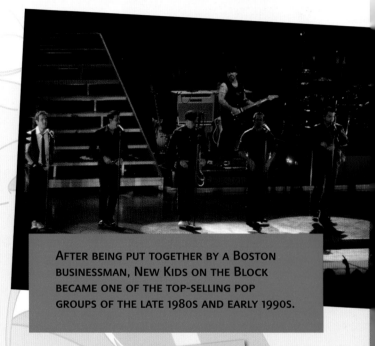

AFTER BEING PUT TOGETHER BY A BOSTON BUSINESSMAN, NEW KIDS ON THE BLOCK BECAME ONE OF THE TOP-SELLING POP GROUPS OF THE LATE 1980S AND EARLY 1990S.

BOY BANDS

Among the most manufactured acts of the time were New Kids on the Block. Formed in 1985 by record producer Maurice Starr, they were the biggest "boy band" of the 1980s. In the UK, a twin-brother band called Bros was huge.

Hangin' Tough

New Kids on the Block was phenomenally successful. After earning their first record contract in 1986, the five school friends from Boston went on to dominate the pop charts. They split up in 1994 after selling over 80 million records worldwide.

MADONNA CONTINUED TO ENJOY SUCCESS IN THE MANUFACTURED POP ERA, THANKS TO HER ABILITY TO TRANSFORM HER LOOK AND SOUND.

HIT FACTORY

Over in the UK, a trio of record producers had set their sights on setting up their own hit factory. Mike Stock, Matt Aitken, and Pete Waterman were the UK's 1980s version of the Motown businessmen of the 1960s.

Puppet Masters

Stock, Aitken, and Waterman became famous for finding fresh talent and producing huge chart hits. They understood pop music and the importance of television as a promotional tool. They even signed actors from popular TV soap operas, such as Kylie Minogue and Jason Donovan, and turned them into pop stars.

Many Hits

Until their decline in the 1990s, Stock, Aitken, and Waterman produced over 100 UK top 40 hits, many of which were also big in the United States. Between them, the trio worked with many successful bands and singers such as Bananarama, Dead or Alive, LaToyah Jackson, Mel & Kim, and Brother Beyond.

BRITISH GIRL GROUP BANANARAMA WERE ONE OF THE MOST SUCCESSFUL ACTS PRODUCED BY HIT-MAKERS STOCK, AITKEN AND WATERMAN.

THE PUPPET MASTERS

The success of manufactured pop acts such as New Kids on the Block between 1988 and 1993 inspired many shrewd businessmen to create their own pop groups. The manager was once again the most important person in pop.

Manufactured Stars

The 1990s and 2000s were a golden age for manufactured pop groups. In Europe, in particular, there was little stopping the success of acts such as Boyzone, Westlife, Take That, and the Spice Girls. Behind each manufactured group was a manager pulling the strings.

BAND BASICS

The idea behind manufactured pop groups is simple. A manager holds an audition, where interested singers get a chance to impress them. After that, a handful of people get picked to be in "the group", and the search for a record deal begins.

Puppet on a String

Most manufactured groups have little say in the songs they play or the clothes they wear. Their manager arranges all this for them. If they are a success, they will become millionaires, as will the manager.

SCOOTER BRAUN MANAGED JUSTIN BIEBER TO INTERNATIONAL SUPERSTARDOM AFTER DISCOVERING HIS VIDEOS ON YOUTUBE WHEN BIEBER WAS ONLY 13 YEARS OLD.

IRISH SUCCESS

Another wildly successful manager was Louis Walsh, an Irishman who decided to put together an Irish rival to Take That. Boyzone and Westlife, the two bands he managed, were a huge success in the UK, Ireland, and New Zealand.

Music Moguls

The 1990s saw the rise of a number of powerful pop managers. Take That, the most successful British boy band of all time, were managed by a former TV casting agent named Nigel Martin-Smith.

Spice Up Your Life

The most successful pop manager of the age, though, was Simon Fuller. The man behind the biggest girl group of the era, the Spice Girls, Fuller built his pop management business into a thriving global empire. Over the years, his acts have notched up 500 number one pop hits around the world.

LIVING LEGENDS

THE SPICE GIRLS

In the late 1990s, the world fell in love with five outspoken British girls and their fun brand of pop music. Their "girl power" message proved so popular with fans that they starred in their own movie, *Spice World*, in 1997. In 2012, they reunited to appear at the closing ceremony of the London Olympics.

IT'S TALENT THAT MATTERS

After dominating the music charts in the 1990s, pop manager Simon Fuller decided to start making TV programs. The shows he came up with revolutionized the relationship between pop and TV.

S Club 7

Fuller's first attempt to take pop to TV was a Monkees-like show about a teen band called *S Club 7*. It was a modest success, being shown in 100 different countries around the world.

Talent Shows Reinvented

Fuller's next idea was simple. He would reinvent an old classic TV format from the past, the talent show. A popular style of program during the 1970s, talent shows allowed ordinary people to showcase their talents—be it singing, dancing, or telling jokes—and win prizes.

POP MANAGER TURNED TV PRODUCER SIMON FULLER WAS GIVEN A STAR ON THE HOLLYWOOD WALK OF FAME IN 2011 IN RECOGNITION OF HIS CONTRIBUTION TO THE ENTERTAINMENT INDUSTRY.

POP IDOL

Fuller's show, *Pop Idol*, was different from '70s talent shows. It offered contestants the chance to win a record deal and a contract with his management agency. Fuller and fellow pop manager Simon Cowell then reaped the rewards when the winner's single skyrocketed to number one.

Reality Bites

Pop Idol launched on British TV in October 2001. It featured a panel of expert judges, including Cowell and pop record producer Pete Waterman. It was a runaway success and helped launch the career of winner Will Young.

SIMON COWELL

Although now known for his TV talent shows, Simon Cowell first made his name in the pop music industry. He worked his way up from the mailroom of major label EMI to become a top executive at BMG Records. During that time, he also managed a number of pop acts, including successful 1980s singer Sinitta.

American Idols

It was in America, though, that Fuller and Cowell's show would become most famous. Remade as *American Idol* by Fox, it became a smash hit and helped turn winners, such as Kelly Clarkson, into massive stars.

Huge Success

Fuller and Cowell followed up the Idol series with a number of other TV talent shows, such as *X Factor* and *America's Got Talent*. Ten years later, reality TV talent shows are as popular as ever. Fuller and Cowell are now among the most powerful men in the entertainment industry.

KELLY CLARKSON SHOT TO FAME AFTER WINNING THE FIRST *AMERICAN IDOL* COMPETITION IN 2002.

URBAN ALL-STARS

While Simon Fuller and Simon Cowell's pop TV talent shows were creating stars, another shift was taking place in pop music. For the first time, two previously underground styles of urban music were dominating the pop charts.

Old Styles, New Sound

By the time they began to become wildly popular in the early 2000s, hip-hop and R & B were already well-established styles of music. Both have their roots in the underground African-American music scene that had once given the world soul and disco.

SINCE FIRST GRACING THE POP CHARTS IN THE 1990S, USHER HAS BECOME THE WORLD'S MOST POPULAR R & B SINGER. TO DATE, HE HAS SOLD OVER 65 MILLION RECORDS.

Black Beats

Over the years, most styles of pop music have in some way grown out of black music culture. Rock and roll, disco, dance music, and even New Wave/synth-pop can trace their roots back to styles of music invented by African Americans. For the most part, though, the styles have been altered to suit white audiences.

SINGER FAITH EVANS IS ONE OF A NEW BREED OF SOUL SINGERS TO ENJOY INTERNATIONAL POP SUCCESS ON THE BACK OF R & B SONGS.

Swing Thing

Hip-hop and R & B were different. For starters, the majority of the scene's stars were African Americans themselves. There was also no need to soften the sound or use white singers, since both black and white teenagers absolutely loved the music.

INSIDE THE SOUND

R&B

R & B as we know it today differs from traditional pop music in many ways. First, it uses loose beats borrowed from hip-hop (as opposed to the rigid beat patterns of dance or New Wave). It also emphasizes the importance of heavy basslines and usually features soulful male or female vocals.

HIP-POP

The first hint of these two urban styles taking over the charts came in 1990, when girl groups TLC and Destiny's Child became huge stars as a result of a sound that mixed R & B and pop. Some time in the early 2000s the dam burst, and suddenly, hip-hop and R & B acts were the biggest pop stars in the world.

RAPPER TURNED BUSINESSMAN SEAN "P. DIDDY" COMBS HELPED MAKE HIP-HOP AND R & B THE MOST POPULAR STYLES OF POP MUSIC AROUND IN THE LATE 1990S AND EARLY 2000S.

Global Sound

Former Destiny's Child singer Beyoncé was the first to climb to the top of the pop music ladder, closely followed by Usher, Missy Elliot, Faith Evans, Jay-Z, and P. Diddy. Since then, many other acts have followed in their footsteps. Even traditional pop singers, such as Madonna and Mariah Carey, have embraced the urban sound of R & B.

TALK ABOUT POP MUSIC

In the twenty-first century, pop music is just as vital and exciting as it has ever been. It continues to react to technological changes and to draw on fresh new influences from other genres. Who knows where it will take us next?

Music on the Move

The Internet has had a huge impact on all areas of our lives, but none more so than the way we access music. Thanks to smartphones, tablet computers, and video sharing sites such as YouTube, we can watch and listen to fresh new pop music whenever we want.

Video Stars

Although the way we access music videos has changed, they're still hugely popular. Record companies still spend huge amounts of money on creating top quality videos, and managers still want their pop groups to appear on popular TV shows.

DOWNLOAD REVOLUTION

The Internet has changed the way we buy music. The days of the 7-inch single, once a staple of pop music, are long gone. Now, we can buy our favorite pop tracks at the push of a button, through online web site and music stores.

RUSSIAN POP SINGER ELKA IS A HUGE STAR IN HER OWN COUNTRY. POP MUSIC IS NOW A TRULY GLOBAL MOVEMENT.

Changes

Pop music itself continues to evolve, too, but often looks to the past. In recent years, top pop stars have enjoyed hits with tracks that sound like '80s New Wave, Motown, and classic dance music. Even R & B stars such as Rihanna and Beyoncé are making dance-pop records.

Global Pop

The biggest change in the last 50 years has been the spread of pop music worldwide. What started out as a variant of underground African-American music in the 1950s has been adopted and adapted by musicians all over the world.

BLACK EYED PEAS STARTED LIFE AS AN UNDERGROUND HIP-HOP CREW BEFORE STORMING UP THE CHARTS WITH A STRING OF POP-DANCE HITS.

Same but Different

Wherever you go in the world, you will find pop music. From South Korea to South America, traditional global musical styles are being mixed with American pop or European dance to create thrilling new fusions. Pop is now a genuine global art form.

KOREAN ARTIST PSY'S *GANGNAM STYLE* MUSIC VIDEO WAS A HUGE HIT ON YOUTUBE AND TO DATE HAS BEEN WATCHED NEARLY 900 MILLION TIMES.

GLOSSARY

album A collection of songs.

art form A type of art, for example, music, painting, or acting.

distinctive Unusual and easily recognized.

drum machine A piece of equipment used by dance and pop artists to create beats and drum patterns.

evolve To change over time.

executive Someone high up in a company, for instance, a director or senior manager.

experimental Music or other art that is born out of trying different or unusual things.

fusion Mixing together two or more different musical styles.

gramophone A piece of equipment used to listen to records.

groundbreaking Important and historic.

manufactured pop A style of pop music created by managers and record labels, featuring singers and dancers who have been handpicked to appeal to teenagers.

masterpiece A great work of art, whether music, painting, or sculpture.

nightclub A place where people go to dance to loud music.

notched up Achieved.

pop A form of upbeat mainstream music. This word is short for "popular".

record A pressed plastic disc featuring recorded music. The forerunner of the CD.

record label A company that specializes in recording and selling pop music.

record producer Someone who specializes in recording songs and making them sound as good as possible.

recording studio The rooms or building used to record and produce music.

revolution An important event or series of events that changes the course of history.

single A musical release featuring one or two pop songs. It can be a record, CD, or digital download.

synthesizer An electronic instrument that looks like a small piano.

thriving Successful.

TV format A style of TV program, for example, a quiz show or soap opera.

underground Not popular and well-known—usually of interest to serious fans only.

vital Lively and important.

FURTHER INFORMATION

Further Reading

From Abba to Zoom: A Pop Culture Encyclopedia of the Late 20th Century by David Mansour (Andrews McMeel Publishing, 2005)

The History of Pop by Ben Hubbard (Crabtree Publishing, 2009)

Justin Bieber (Superstars!) by Lynn Peppas (Crabtree Publishing, 2011)

Kidz Bop: Be a Pop Star!: Start Your Own Band, Book Your Own Gigs, and Become a Rock and Roll Phenom! by Kimberly Potts (Adams Media, 2011)

Web Sites

www.billboard.com/charts/hot-100
Find out what's topping the U.S. pop charts this week. The site also contains loads of great facts and figures about previous U.S. chart-toppers.

http://www.factmonster.com/ipka/A0885982.html
All you need to know about 250 years of American popular music history, in one easy timeline.

www.rollingstone.com/music/lists/the-500-greatest-songs-of-all-time-20110407
The stories behind the 500 greatest pop and rock songs of all time, picked by America's leading music magazine, Rolling Stone.

www.youtube.com/music/pop
Watch the latest music videos and classic clips from years gone by.

INDEX